Todd is one of the top mortga[...] really no surprise that he would come up with a great book like this. The material digs deep behind the scenes of a home loan, and will help any consumer understand how things really work…and learn how they can use this knowledge for their own best interest. Anyone considering buying or refinancing a home—or even anyone interested in expanding their learning base—will gain a great deal of value from this down-to-earth, super informative read.

Sue Woodard
VP Mortgage Market Guide

I believe education relating to mortgage financing is so critical to today's consumer. For most, a mortgage is the largest debt a person will incur in their life and the home is the largest asset. This book is a great resource to help answer the must-know questions when acquiring a mortgage.

Jim McMahan
Division Vice President
CTX Mortgage Co.

The Borrower's Bible

WRITTEN BY:

TODD J. GEHRKE

The Borrower's Bible

Published by arrangement with Dramatrapolis and Dog Ear Publishing

Copyright© 2006 by Todd J. Gehrke

All rights reserved. No part of this publication may be reproduced, stored in a retrieval system, or transmitted, in any form or by any means, electronic, mechanical, photocopying, recording, or otherwise, without the written prior permission of the author. Contact the author at:

Artwork by Robert Hay

Edited by Briana Selstad

Published by Dog Ear Publishing
4010 W. 86th Street, Ste H
Indianapolis, IN 46268
Visit our websites at:
www.dogearpublishing.net
www.baloaney.com

ISBN: 1-59858-217-8

Library of Congress Control Number: 2006934418

This book is printed on acid-free paper.

Printed in the United States of America

TABLE OF CONTENTS

INTRODUCTION

Knowledge is power? Not hardly...not on its own anyways. I believe that knowledge plus *interpretation* plus *action equals real power. And in my twenty plus years of working in the mortgage business, I've seen over and over how clients could benefit from this combination...often resulting in saving them literally hundreds of thousands of dollars. And from my extensive work in national television and media, I've seen the massive amount of misinformation that is delivered on a daily basis, by those who simply do not understand. All too often, raw facts or knowledge are not accompanied by interpretation, nor is a clear course of action devised by a trusted advisor.*

In this book, Todd Gehrke has drawn upon some of the greatest minds in the industry to provide you with the knowledge—and better yet, the clear interpretation—to really understand what happens behind the scenes of a home loan. How and why do home loan rates change? What really impacts your credit score? What are lenders really looking at when they make their approval decision? Does looking back at the his-

tory of rates really provide us with a glimpse into the future? This book will provide all those answers and more. And to determine your own course of action for a home loan and financial strategy, Todd is one of the leading home loan consultants in the nation. After reading this book, look no further to help apply your knowledge and interpretation, and learn the actions you can take today...that may impact your wealth for the rest of your life.

All the best—

Barry Habib
CEO, Mortgage Market Guide

FOREWORD

Why did I write this book?

In 1999 I bought my first home with my new wife from a large national homebuilder. Actually, my wife bought it. I didn't have a good enough credit score. I didn't have a BAD score, I had NO score. I grew up in northern Wisconsin where I was taught that if you didn't have the money in your pocket, you couldn't afford it. Somehow I managed through college without being seduced into a credit card and accumulated zero debt by graduation. When I applied for the mortgage, I remember asking (or exclaiming) "Do you mean, because I have always been able to save up money to buy things instead of borrow money when I couldn't afford something I want, that now that I need to do so I am unqualifiable?!? Because I have NO DEBT, I do not prove that I can manage debt?!?"

And his answer: "Exactly."

We bought a nice three bedroom, two and one half bath tri-level home across the street from an elementary school. I naively remember thinking to myself, "We plan on having two kids, so there will be a bedroom for each of the kids and the master for us. The kids will go to school right across the

street, and we will live happily ever after. After all, I lived in one house all through my youth until I graduated from high school, why wouldn't my kids?"

That thinking dictated my decision for a 30-year fixed mortgage. Our "Loan Officer" was a representative of the builder, and treated the mortgage as the necessary means to the sale, offering no advice or counsel. His only question to us as first time homebuyers was, "Do you want an adjustable mortgage or a fixed rate?" Knowing nothing of either, the thought of an adjustable rate did not seem good, so we opted for a fixed. Sadly, in the five years that we lived in that house we had three different mortgages, rolling the costs into the loan each time and paying points to boot, needlessly losing over $12,000 on our mortgage of $150,000. My estimates show a loss of nearly 8% of the total mortgage on poor decisions due to a lack of information.

Just as you do, I work hard for the money I earn. The last thing I ever want to do is squander it away due to incompetence. I wrote this book after years of counseling homebuyers and homeowners on liability management. This book is reflective of my views and should be read to stimulate your thoughts and opinions. Challenge what you read here, create your own views. My goal is that you will be able to make more knowledgeable decisions with your finances as a result of what you learn in the pages to follow.

As Benjamin Disraeli stated in the early 1800's:

"As a general rule the most successful man in life is the man who has the best information."

Enjoy *The Borrower's Bible*.
Sincerely,

Todd J. Gehrke
Loan Ranger
www.baloaney.com

KEY COMPONENTS OF A MORTGAGE

Acquiring a mortgage can be boiled down to three essential phases: credit, DTI (Debt to Income), and CLTV (Combined Loan to Value). In this section we will break each down and discuss solutions to improve your ability to receive financing at the lowest possible cost and rate.

PHASE ONE: UNDERSTANDING CREDIT

"A good reputation is more valuable than money."

Publilius Syrus (~100 BC)

The first phase we will discuss is credit. When applying for a mortgage a tri-bureau credit report is pulled. A tri-bureau credit report consists of a report from each of the three bureaus: Equifax, Experian and Trans Union merged into one report. Your "score" will be the middle, or median, score of the three—not an average of the three. Currently the average middle score in America is in the 680's. Credit scores consider a wide range of information on your credit report. However, they do not consider:

• Your race, color, religion, national origin, sex and marital status. United States law prohibits credit scoring from considering these facts, as well as any receipt of public assistance, or the exercise of any consumer right under the Consumer Credit Protection Act.

- Your age. Other types of scores may consider your age, but credit scores don't.

- Your salary, occupation, title, employer, date employed, or employment history. Lenders may consider this information, however, as may other types of scores.

- Where you live.

- Any interest rate being charged on a particular credit card or other account.

- Any items reported as child/family support obligations or rental agreements.

- Certain types of inquiries (requests for your credit report). The score does not count "consumer-initiated" inquiries—requests you have made for own your credit report. It also does not count "promotional inquiries"—requests made by lenders in order to make you a "pre-approved" credit offer, or "administrative inquiries," requests made by lenders to review your account with them. Requests that are marked as coming from employers are not counted either.

- Any information not found in your credit report.

- Any information that is not proven to be predictive of future credit performance.

- Any non-financial information, like if you had your Wheaties for breakfast this morning.

Isn't that perfect? This is the one area where how you look and who you know has no bearing. The world is fair and on an even playing field. Each person directs his/her own destiny and will stand up and be accountable for their own actions. No one cares what color your hair is, how much you weigh, or what grade you got in 10th grade algebra.

It is important to understand the concept of credit, why it exists, and who the credit companies work for. Your credit score serves as nothing more than a report card of your financial responsibility when borrowing money. The "scorers" are the three major credit bureaus that gather data, for a fee, from anyone that wants to provide them information about you. The reason lending companies i.e.: VISA, MasterCard, mortgage companies, banks, etc. are willing to pay these compa-

nies for this task is because it will help them assess the risk involved with lending you their money. That is simple enough; the flaw however, has evolved through the dependency of this score. Since lenders will charge you a rate based on a score, there is a general concern that they have a motive to process their data in certain ways that result in lowering your score, so they can justifiably charge you higher interest. For example, the amount you owe on a credit card (balance) compared to the amount you can borrow (limit on that card) makes up 30% of your score (as noted in the graph ahead). One such practice common with most credit card companies is to record your limit as the highest balance you have ever had instead of the actual limit on the card. What this means is, if you had a credit card with a $10,000 limit, but have never exceeded a $2,000 balance, your recorded limit with the bureaus would be $2,000. If you bought a new Hi Definition TV over the weekend with that card for $1,999, you would appear to have maxed out your card, and your score would drop—even though you still had $8,000 left! Another subtle variance is the day that the credit card company reports to the bureaus. I have many clients that use their credit cards to rack up airline miles but pay the card off in full each month. They are always curious as to why their credit cards show a balance when we pull credit. A common assumption is that the credit bureaus report your current balance the day after your due date so they can record if you made a timely payment or a late payment. That is not always the case. Many credit card companies report to the bureaus approximately ten days before your payment is due. Why? There is no proof of their intention, but it is a common assumption that even if you pay off your card in full, the period of time that your card would show the highest possible balance would be BEFORE the due date, not after. Therefore, whether intentional or not, by reporting seven to ten days before the payment due date, there is a greater opportunity that your score will be lower.

The lower your score, the higher your rates.

Read on, there are things you can do.

YOUR CREDIT

Credit scores are calculated from a lot of different credit data in your credit report. This data can be grouped into five categories as outlined below. The percentages in the chart reflect how important each of the categories is in determining your score.

Components that influence your credit, for better or worse:

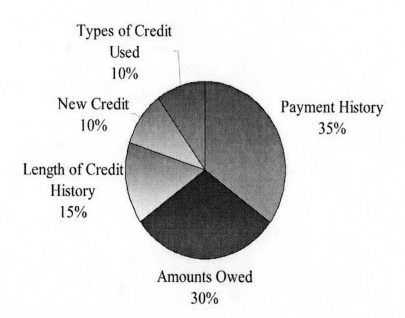

PAYMENT HISTORY

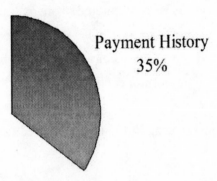

Payment History
35%

    The largest factor in a credit report is your payment history. On the positive side a responsible, timely payment history demonstrates a low credit risk. On the negative side, late payments, accounts in collections, public records such as judgments or bankruptcies, and so forth can play a damaging role. A combination of negative and positive figures makes your payment history account for nearly 35% of your credit score.

HOW TO FIX NEGATIVE PAYMENT HISTORY:

Let me preface this chapter with my personal belief. If you owe money, be responsible and pay it back. That is the right thing to do. With that said, I will explain how to eliminate derogatory information from your credit report regardless if it is accurate or inaccurate. Do not expect credit bureaus to make it easy for you.

We will start with the hard way. If you do have derogatory information on your report, there are things you can do. For accounts in collections and public records such as judgments or bankruptcies, DO NOT JUST PAY THEM!!! Contact each bureau individually and request a copy of their report, which will cost you about $20. Then dispute all derogatory information, simply stating that it is an error on your report, and that you would like them to investigate the error and have it removed. That will start a chain of events in which the bureau will contact the entity that reported the derogatory item requesting proof that you were at fault. The entity in question has 30 days to respond to the inquiry. If they fail to do so, the bureau will simply delete the item—problem solved.

Why does this often work? And why don't you want to just pay it off? Let's address the second question first. Time heals all wounds. The longer you have had an outstanding debt the less of a negative impact it will have on your credit report, until it finally drops off in seven to ten years. If you have a medical collection, or cell phone bill (those are the most common) that is four years old and you pay it, you may be bringing that account from outstanding to paid in full (good) but you are also taking a derogatory account that has "healed" for four years and opening it up again with your new activity updated to today, starting the whole "healing process" over again (bad). After all, it still is a debt that you paid four years late, that is not exactly good. So why can you get away with disputing it and denying that it was ever yours? In a nut shell, bad bookkeeping and labor costs. Even a bankruptcy can be eliminated from your credit report because of their bookkeeping policy. Here is a common scenario for illustration: A medical billing company's policy states that two years after the outstanding bill has gone without payment the facility copies your billing documents onto a microfiche and takes them to a storage facility to sit for an additional five years. If the credit bureaus send a letter to the medical billing company disputing that you received treatment, but failed to pay the full balance, the medical billing company would then need to pay a worker to go to the storage facility, search the endless mass of records just to be able to report back to state that you did have an outstanding balance four years ago that has already been written off as bad debt. For that, the medical billing company receives no financial benefit, and there would be no additional fees because after all, no one is taking legal action—you are just asking them to do more work. So they don't. If they do go through the work, and do state that—yes, in fact you did have a file years ago, what do you do? File another dispute. All they need to do is miss the deadline of 30 days once and your problem is solved. This works with most old collections.

For more recent bad debts that you would like to settle, DO NOT JUST PAY THEM. Sticking with the "time heals all wounds" concept, it is very important that you pay them in a specific manner in order to help, not hurt your credit score. First of all, you do have room to negotiate these outstanding debts and pay less than the recorded balance. Most companies write these off as bad debt expenses after a certain time period and eventually sell them to collection companies at pennies on the dollar. Once the collection company owns the debt, you have an opportunity to negotiate with them. If the collection company pays ten cents for every dollar that you owe, you have an opportunity to pay them half of your outstanding balance or less as a payment in full! The key here is the method of negotiation, and the specific verbiage used to make sure that once the debt is settled, it does not adversely affect your credit score. Here are some guidelines:

1. As a general rule, negotiate with collection companies at the end of a month. Most follow a traditional calendar with sales records. They have quotas to fill just like car dealerships, and the end of the month is the perfect time to help them make their numbers.

2. Ask the right questions. Why waste time negotiating with someone who does not have the ability to settle the claim? Start by asking this question: **"Do you have the authority to settle this claim today**

at less than the outstanding balance?" If they say no, ask them to connect you with someone who does. Keep climbing the ladder until you are speaking with someone that can. Everyone else is wasting your time!

3. Be ready to pay immediately. "A bird in the hand is worth two in the bush." As soon as you get an agreeable price, be ready (and able) to pay it on the spot. That will help in your negotiating process. There are some great books on negotiation that will help you set the stage to win. I personally recommend "Start with NO" by Jim Camp and "Getting to Yes" by Roger Fisher and William Ury.

4. Do not pay without getting a guarantee in writing that this amount will deem the balance paid in full and that this action will result in NO ADVERSE AFFECT to your credit report. Get this in writing BEFORE sending them payment. The verbiage here is of the utmost importance. You want them to delete this account from their records if at all possible. Then when you go to dispute the derogatory later on you have a letter from the company stating that you do not have a record with the company, resulting in a deleted derogatory.

I did say there was an easier way. If you do not want to go through the laborious task of contacting all three bureaus, filing disputes to all three bureaus for each derogatory item, researching and training to become a master negotiator, jumping into the ring to go rounds with debt collectors and then acting on your behalf as a make-shift attorney to make sure at the end of it all you pay the debt and it truly does not hurt your credit, there is a very easy solution. Contact credit mediators that specialize in handling everything I just discussed and more. Mediators range in service, effectiveness, and costs. The company I personally recommend charges a ridiculously low fee (in my opinion) to start the process, then per month until you don't need them anymore—no contracts. Expect to hire them for a full six months minimum to get the results needed. You can reach them at <u>www.baloaney.com</u> under the "CREDIT ISSUES?" link on the upper right-hand corner of the home page. When you visit mention that Todd sent you, they will take great care of you and their service is well worth the money.

AMOUNTS OWED—REVOLVING DEBT (CREDIT CARDS)

Amounts Owed
30%

The use of your revolving credit is also important. Revolving credit is short-term and varies from month to month. Credit cards are one example. If you carry a balance on one or more cards, your score may drop. How much your score goes up or down depends on your balance versus maximum limit. Using more than about one-third of your maximum credit may lower your credit rating—and revolving credit accounts for about 30–35% of your credit score.

When calculating your balance to limit ratio, simply divide your balance by the limit listed on the credit report. If the number you get is greater than .30, your score receives a deduction. If you get a number greater than .50, your score receives another deduction. Remember—this applies to each card individually, not your total balance to limit combined. One of the easiest ways to improve your credit score is to measure each credit card individually and get them all below 50%. For example: If you have three cards. One is a Discover that has a $15,000 limit and is nearly maxed out with a balance of $14,000 because you receive a 0% interest rate for six months. You have a Visa that has a $10,000 limit, and a MasterCard with a $5,000 limit that both have zero balances. Your score will be higher if you transfer $4,900 onto the Visa and $1,166 onto the MasterCard. Now EACH card has a balance to limit ratio of less than 50%.

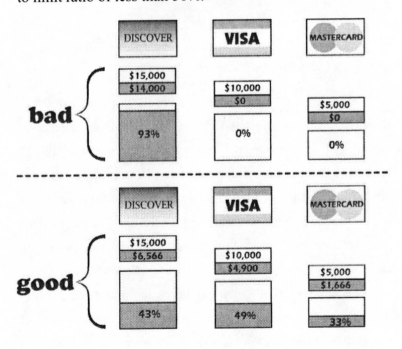

LENGTH IN YEARS OF YOUR CREDIT HISTORY

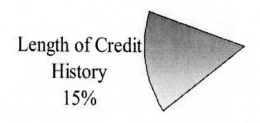

Length of Credit History 15%

Another factor is the length in years of your credit history. The longer you demonstrate responsible credit management, the higher your credit score. On the other hand, negative credit information can hurt your score for years, though older data is less damaging than recent activity. Many consumers are surprised when their credit score drops because they "did the right thing" and paid down an old, inactive debt (See PAYMENT HISTORY). Credit history amounts to about 15% of your score. What this means is, do not close any old open accounts—doing so will hurt your score. Even some of the old store-specific credit cards to the Gap or Limited that you opened in college are affecting your score. You may never use it again (and it is a bad idea to open an account like that in the first place), but if it is open, leave it open. If you decide you want to rid yourself of credit cards, start with the most recently opened cards first. By closing the "young" ones, you can increase the average length of your accounts, thus increasing your credit score.

TYPES OF CREDIT USED

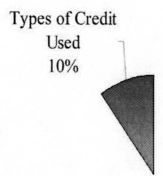

Types of Credit
Used
10%

10% of your credit score is based on the ways in which you use credit. If you have five credit cards extending $10,000 in credit total, this may lower or raise your score compared to financing a single $10,000 installment loan. Typically, higher credit scores demonstrate responsible use of multiple account types (I.E. both installment loans and revolving credit). The perfect mix includes a mortgage, a car loan, and three long-established credit cards in good standing with low balances.

NEW CREDIT

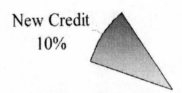

New Credit
10%

Finally, "new credit" covers about 10% of your score. New accounts have not yet had time to prove responsibility and slightly damage a score per an "inquiry" made. Multiple new accounts can predict a financial risk crisis. Very large extensions of credit, like a home loan or new vehicle loan, can reduce your ability to get more credit in the short term. For example, if you opened four credit cards in the same month, you would see a drop in your credit score.

The lower the credit score, the higher the risk to the investor, the higher the interest rate.

PHASE TWO: CALCULATING DTI (DEBT TO INCOME)

CAUTION: This is Math. The formulas written in this section are simple, but it is math. Do not get bogged down in this chapter and stop reading the book. If math is not your thing, skim this chapter and move on.

There are two types of Debt to Income, simply called front and back. The front DTI determines how much of your monthly income is consumed by your mortgage payment. The calculation for front DTI is your total mortgage payment divided by your gross (before tax) monthly income.

Total Mortgage Payment

(divided by)

Gross (before tax) monthly income

Your back DTI will be your total mortgage payment plus all monthly payments indicated on your credit report plus any alimony/child support divided by your gross (before tax) monthly income. Or how much of your monthly income is consumed by all of your outstanding debts.

Total Mortgage Payment
+ all monthly payments indicated on your credit report
+ any alimony/child support
(divided by)
Gross (before tax) monthly income

Ratios vary depending on the type of loan you are applying for and the investor's specific guidelines. In the example below the ratios are 28/45 **(45% back end is the maximum for most "A" paper, or for most investors that will give you the lowest rates)**, meaning a front ratio of 28 and a back ratio of 45. In the illustration following the front end ratio equals 25, by dividing the $2,000 total mortgage payment by the $8,000 in monthly income. The back ratio equals 31.25 by adding the total mortgage payment of $2,000 to the monthly debts of $500 and then dividing that total ($2500) by the monthly income of $8,000. NOTE: Total monthly payment includes taxes and insurance. If you are buying a town home or condo, it will also include the Home Owners Association Dues.

The higher the DTI, the higher the risk to the investor—and the higher the interest rate.

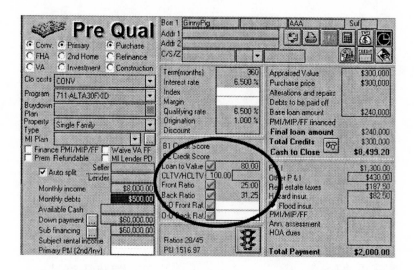

PHASE THREE: CLTV (COMBINED LOAN TO VALUE)

Combined Loan to Value means what the total of all mortgages equals in relation to the value or price of the property, whichever is least. In the previous example we can see that the buyer is buying a home priced at $300,000 and has a loan to value of 80% with a loan amount of $240,000. In addition he has a second mortgage of $60,000 which equals 20% of the price of the home, and makes his combined loan to value (80+20) 100%. The higher the CLTV, the higher the risk to the investor—and the higher the interest rate.

Understanding the three elements of credit, DTI and CLTV gives you the basic principles that investors use when assessing risk to your financing—in other words, determining your rate.

MORTGAGE INSURANCE

Looking at CLTV a little closer, and adding in the principle of mortgage insurance, imagine if you were an investor with money to lend. One day you are approached by Bob and Shirley Snombrowski, whom you did not previously know. Bob has managed a retail store in the area for three years and Shirley is going on her third year as a teacher for a local junior high school (EMPLOYMENT HISTORY). Bob has a profit sharing retirement plan he qualified for last year and has already acquired about $1,200 in retirement funds and Shirley's school retirement program shows a balance of almost $3,000 (RESERVES). They have always shown a pretty good willingness to repay (CREDIT SCORE), and have good jobs and nothing more than one car loan and a couple small credit cards, which you consider strong proof of their ability to repay (DTI). They asked to borrow $100,000 to purchase a $100,000 house.

Now, you believe that they are going to repay you plus interest, but still need to look at the security of the investment. The "what if they don't" part. You decide to draw it out to see if it all makes sense. On a sheet of paper you draw a rectangle representing the $100,000 house, the value.

$100,000 Investment

You then color in the portion that equals your investment. Because they are equal, you now have one gray rectangle.

100%

What if...

All goes well for a couple years, then all of the sudden the Snombrowskis quit paying you back. You start sending them notices requesting them to get current and do not get a response (or a check). You hire a company to help collect the money and the phone number is disconnected. After several months of inactivity and no payments, your investment (The Snombrowskis) with a pretty good willingness to re-pay (CREDIT SCORE) and strong proof of their ability to re-pay (DTI), seems to be a bust. You need to start getting your money back. The taxes are not getting paid; your investment portfolio is taking a major hit. You are oblivious to the fact that, tragically, Bob lost his job and can no longer find work. Since he is a mid-level manager in a retail environment, he is being replaced by kids half his age that are willing to work for half as much. He is physically unable to work a labor position and his education has been hands-on, with no formal degree. He has considered going back to school, but with what money? Savings kept them afloat for a while, but they eventually ran out, leaving Shirley on her teacher's salary to cover the bills alone. With the savings gone and the bills stacking up, Bob and Shirley have nowhere to turn, and you need to foreclose on them. The foreclosure process will take a minimum of nine months. All the while you are not getting paid on your investment, the taxes on your property are not getting paid, and the collateral of your investment is dropping. You lost 5% of the value of your investment evicting your borrowers.

95%

Finally you are able to get into "your" house, so you can get it ready to sell only to discover that the strangers you let live there were not altogether pleased about getting kicked out, and decided they were going to take anything of value, or at least destroy it so you couldn't have it. Since they have been thrown onto the street in their greatest moment of need, they decided to throw every light fixture onto the street as well; Bob's brother took the ceiling fans, the washer and dryer, and the fridge. He even took the toilet from the downstairs bathroom! Then, after they moved in with Shirley's parents out-of-state, some of Shirley's 6th graders, who were told that the banker for the house kicked them out when they needed help most, rode their bikes by one evening and threw rocks through the front windows. You don't know the story, all you know is that your investment is losing money fast, and you just lost another chunk of cash, at least 5%.

90%

Now it is time to put this god awful thing back on the market. You interview realtors and realize that any way you slice it; it will run you about 7% to get the house sold. In other words, there goes another $6,300 of the $90,000 left.

83.7%

Based on this all too common consideration, you tell the Snombrowskis that you will lend them 100% of the money they need under one condition. They must acquire and pay for a mortgage insurance policy with you as the beneficiary for the top 20% of your investment. That way, even if they get into trouble, you are covered because your insurance carries beyond your established "danger zone." It will cost them a little more, but they will be able to get the house they want with little to nothing down, and they go for it—the house is theirs.

Or maybe they don't agree. You see, the "problem" with the insurance is that you are paying for more than you are borrowing, and the insurance (as of 2006) is not tax deductible. So, knowing that they need to pay an insurance policy for anything over 80%, (and they do not have enough money to put 20% of their own money into the deal) the Snombrowskis contact another investor such as yourself to borrow the additional 20%. Thus having all the money they need, 80% from you, plus 20% from another source, equaling the 100% they need to buy the house. Let's look at the risk level our 20% lender incurs. If the overall loss on 100% equals roughly 17% off the top, then that equals 85% of the top 20%! That's some risk! How does investor B compensate for that risk? Simple. He charges for it. The Snombrowskis pay for it in higher rates. That's OK though, don't get the impression that it is not. Higher risk should incur higher rates. IT STILL in most cases has a lower over-all cost than paying mortgage insurance. After all, 100% plus mortgage insurance equals a sum greater than 100%; 80% plus 20% only equals 100%—it's still less.

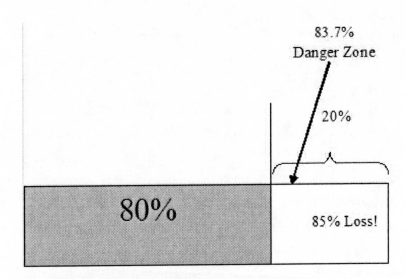

So your fine candidates return to you requesting 100% of the money they need in the form of an 80/20 loan. And they have asked you if you would be willing to charge them interest-only on the $80,000.

INTEREST-ONLY OPTION LOANS

There are different theories behind interest-only option loans, this is only one of them. If you have two piles of money, one pile charging you six cents per dollar (6%) and another charging you nine cents per dollar (9%), which pile would you like to get rid of first? (Hint, common sense will tell you that you should pick the 9% one.) If you do pick the 9% one, then why would you pay anything towards the cheaper debt until the more expensive debt is paid off? You wouldn't. Enter the interest-only option mortgage. The goal is to lock in the lowest cost possible for the longest time needed on the cheaper pile of money, the 80%, and pay all you can to the higher cost debt. Keep in mind, this is called an interest-only OPTION loan, not interest-only loan. You CAN, at any time, pay toward principle—but it is always your choice. Not unlike a credit card, you always have a minimum payment due, which you must pay to avoid penalties, but you CAN pay any amount above that up to the full balance. As an over-all debt strategy, you need to look at all of your incurred debts and their subsequent interest rates. It is the most cost-effective to pay down the smallest balances first, and the highest rates first. In nearly all cases that will not be your mortgage.

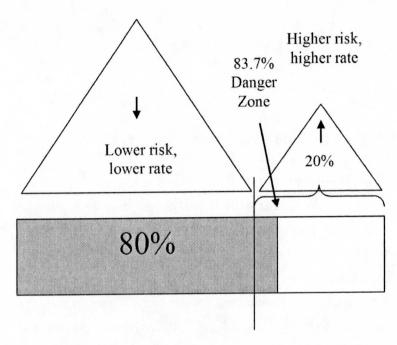

Think about your mortgage as any other debt you have. If you have two mortgages (possibly to avoid mortgage insurance, for example) you have two entirely different piles of money—one large pile, with very low risk to the investor and a low interest rate, and the other smaller pile at a higher risk, thus a higher rate. In an ordinary situation you would be inclined to pay off the smaller pile first if for no other reason than because that pile, dollar for dollar, is costing you more money.

By choosing an interest-only loan on the first (lower cost) mortgage, you reduce the overall cost to you by allocating that additional payment to the second mortgage and paying it off faster.

THE GENERAL DIFFERENCE BETWEEN TRADITIONAL AND INTEREST-ONLY LOANS

Below is a diagram showing the difference between a traditional mortgage and an interest-only option mortgage.

Imagine that the box below represents a 30-year mortgage term. We know statistically that most people, on average, sell and buy a new home today once every six years (National Association of Realtors)*. The way traditional principle and interest mortgage loans are amortized, the majority of the payment in the first 21 years is interest, with very little being applied toward principle. With that being the case, assume that the diagonal line drawn across the diagram represents the decreasing interest over the years. I have indicated where the 5-year marker is over a 30-year term to illustrate how much principle (blackened area) is actually being paid by the average homeowner in a 5-year period.

The dotted line represents the same loan, but where the payment would be if choosing an interest-only option. The reason people are being swayed towards interest-only loans is because the value of one's home will go up (or down) regardless of what one owes on the property, therefore, in an interest-only option loan, they have the option of paying more, but the flexibility of paying less than a traditional amortized mortgage.

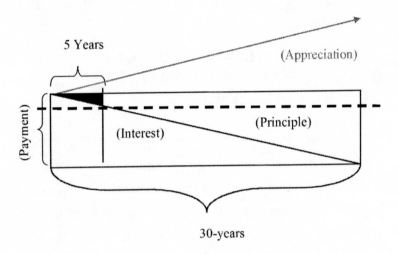

FORMULA:

$$\left(\frac{\text{PRINCIPLE BALANCE * RATE}}{\text{12 MONTHS}} \right) = \text{MONTHLY PAYMENT}$$

Let's look at it another way. Imagine that you are looking at a standard eight-foot long 2- by 4-inch board, like the one below. The eight feet represent the length of time of your mortgage (30-years). The height of two inches represents your monthly payment.

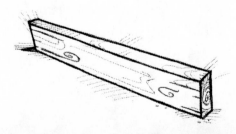

The difference is that your view is simply the two inches by four inches, and the board is sticking eight feet straight out in front of your face, like the diagram on the following page. This view represents your monthly mortgage payment.

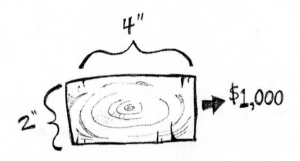

If you had a traditional 30-year fixed mortgage, and you decided to pay off half of your remaining loan balance, the banker would walk eight feet away from you and cut off the last four feet of your board.

You would effectively reduce the length of time that you would owe them money. However, the view of your monthly obligation (the payment) would not change. Next month you would still owe them the same dollar amount, and your payment would still look like this.

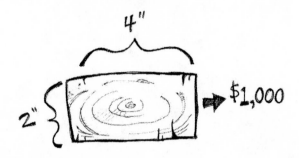

Now let's say you chose the same loan, but selected an interest-only option instead and decided to pay off half of your remaining loan balance, instead of walking to the back of your loan, and stepping off four feet, the banker would start right in front of you and make a cut right down the center of your board all the way down eight feet (essentially shaving off the top one inch).

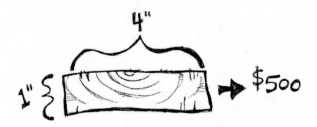

Now the view of your monthly payment has changed dramatically: it has been reduced to half the size. So the following month you would literally owe half as much in a mortgage payment, as well as half the mortgage amount.

DETERMINING YOUR HIGHEST COST DEBT

The title of this section seems to be a blinding flash of the obvious doesn't it? I'm sure you have already said to yourself, "Wouldn't that be the balance with the highest rate?" If you did, the answer would be NO—NOT NECESSARILY. There are too many ways to calculate the impact that taxes have on our overall financial position. The general rule when determining the effect taxes have on your monthly bills is simple. Once you have determined your taxed rate (www.irs.gov), simply take the interest rate of your mortgage and subtract your income tax rate to determine your net cost (the cost after your tax deduction).

Example:

Interest Rate = 6.5%
Tax Bracket = 25%
6.5–25% = 4.875%

Or,

[100–25%=75%] 6.5 * .75 = 4.875%

By understanding this, you understand that a car loan at 5% still costs you more than a mortgage at 6.5%, and the car loan should be paid off before applying anything towards the mortgage. If you believe in this concept, there is a great possibility that the only time you will begin paying off your mortgage is when you have no other outstanding debts. Even student loans, which usually carry low interest rates and have limited tax deductibility, may be better off paid before the mortgage, depending on your income tax bracket.

INTEREST-ONLY—Why else?

OK, on to the velocity of money principle, or money in motion. Picture a dollar that is in your wallet. While it is stagnating, does it have any value to you at all? No. A dollar has no value until you become a consumer and use it to purchase some type of product or service. The following is an example of money in motion: a dollar is passed from you to a business, which uses it to compensate an employee in the form of wages. That earned dollar is spent at the grocery store. The grocer then uses that dollar to cover the cost of produce inventory from the wholesaler. The wholesaler then pays the farmer for the produce, who in turn uses it for a new tractor for harvesting the produce. The manufacturer of the tractor then uses that same dollar for operating the machinery that builds the tractor. Notice how quickly the dollar moves from one hand to the other?

Now, let's examine how this concept of money in motion ultimately generates profits. The banking industry has mastered the art of money in motion so well that it makes sense to use them as an example. When you deposit money into a Certificate of Deposit (CD), let's say $10,000, and you earn in the neighborhood of 2% to 3%. What do you suppose then happens with that money? They invest a portion of it in the form of loans back to the public. If you have a car loan, home equity loan, etc. with the bank, is it at 2–3%? Of course not! The bank has leveraged the money they have collected in deposits and loaned it back out to others creating a concept of "arbitrage." They PAY 2–3% for the money, but COLLECT 8–10% for that same money at the exact same time. Thus profiting the difference (no wonder bankers have so much money!). If they took that money and left it secured in the safe, it would COST money, instead of EARN money. This is important for you to understand because you have an opportunity with your mortgage to secure very low rates on your mortgage. You will be able to borrow more, and earn higher rates of return on the borrowed money in terms of retirement savings. For more information regarding the Velocity of Money, please reference the book Missed Fortune by Douglas Andrew, or any mortgage professional that is a Mortgage Market Guide subscriber that has attended an Equity Management Summit and is a Certified Mortgage Planning Specialist™.

UNDERSTANDING WHAT INFLUENCES RATES

WHAT ARE BONDS?

Bonds are fancy IOUs.

Companies and governments issue bonds to fund their day-to-day operations or to finance specific projects. When you buy a bond, you are loaning your money for a certain period of time to the issuer, be it General Electric or Uncle Sam. In return, bond holders get back the loan amount plus interest payments. Mortgage-backed securities are debt obligations that represent claims to the cash flows from pools of mortgage loans, most commonly on residential property.

In exchange, the borrower promises to pay you interest every year and to return your principal at maturity, when the loan comes due. The length of time to maturity called the term.

A bond's face value, or price at issue, is known as its par value. Its interest payment is known as its coupon.

A $1,000 bond paying 7% per year has a $70 coupon (actually, the money would usually arrive in two $35 payments spaced six months apart). Expressed another way, its coupon rate is 7%. If you buy the bond for $1,000 and hold it to maturity, the annual yield, or actual earnings on your investment, is also 7% (coupon divided by price = yield).

The prices of bonds fluctuate throughout the trading day, as do their yields. But the coupon payments stay the same.

Say you don't buy the bond right at the offering, and instead buy from somebody else in the secondary market. If you buy the bond for $1,100 in the secondary market, the coupon will still be $70, but the yield is 6.4% ($70/$1,100) because you paid a premium for the bond.

For a similar reason, if you buy it for $900, its yield will be 7.8% ($70/$900) because you bought the bond at a discount. If its current price equals its face value, the bond is said to be selling at par.

INFLATION AND GAS PRICES COMPARED TO A BOND'S RATE AND YIELD

You are at home watching "Lilo and Stitch" on the Disney Channel with your kids on a Saturday morning when the doorbell rings. When you answer the door, there is a young man in jeans and a red golf shirt with a local gas station's name printed on the left chest. He quickly starts his pitch.

"Sir, I am from the corner gas station and am going door to door because we made a mistake and you get to profit by buying a $150 gas debit card for $100."

Your immediate reaction of distaste for door to door salespeople is abruptly diverted by his statement.

"Say again?" you respond as you suddenly realize that you are in a white stained T-shirt and some flannel pants you got in college that you slept in last night.

"I said, I am from the corner gas station and am going door to door because we made a mistake and you get to profit by buying a $150 gas debit card for $100."

"What is the catch?"

"No catch sir." He replies. "The reason we are selling them for $100 is that our promotion starts at the beginning of next month and our printer misprinted them with next years date, so they will not be valid until next year at this time. It's a great deal to you though. You get to make a 50% return on your investment. We thought since you live in the area and are coming to our store anyway, we would offer this to you as kind of a reward."

Now, you may not be a mathematician, but that sounds like a pretty good deal! So you jump on it.

Of course, if you were a mathematician, or an economist, you would have thought about it a little more carefully.

First of all, the price of the gas card represents a bond that will mature in one year. The "yield" is the $50 that that bond will return upon maturity.

The X factor in determining if this is a good investment is simply this…

How many gallons of gas will $100 buy now, vs. how much will $150 buy next year?

Let's assume this scenario is taking place in the early summer of 2005. (I guess they would be flannel boxers instead of pants then, but follow along anyway!) Gas prices were right around $2 per gallon. $100 divided by $2 equals 50 gallons of gas. But by September of 2005, gas prices rose (inflation) to a national average of $3.07 per gallon.* At that time $150 worth of gas would equal 48.86 gallons of gas ($150 divided by $3.07). You would have LOST 1.14 gallons of gas! Not to mention tied up $100 worth of your money for one year! (GAS PRICE RESOURCE: Steve Stoft, Ph.D. economist http://zfacts.com)

PRICE, RATE AND YIELD

So, being the numbers genius that you are, you explain to your savvy salesman that this is not a very good deal, because you are afraid that gas prices are going to rise too much over the next year (inflation). Now the bargaining begins. You are interested in buying a card though, so you offer him $80. After some back and forth, you strike a deal at $85. What happened? The PRICE of the card, or bond, decreased to $85 and the YIELD of the card, or bond, increased to $65.

Mortgage rates align with yield. As prices go down, yield (rates) goes up. The following illustration shows the price and yield of a 5-year treasury note.

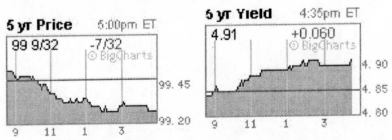

Do you notice that the charts are an exact mirror image of each other? Look what happens if you flip over yield chart and lay it directly on top of the price chart: they look the same.

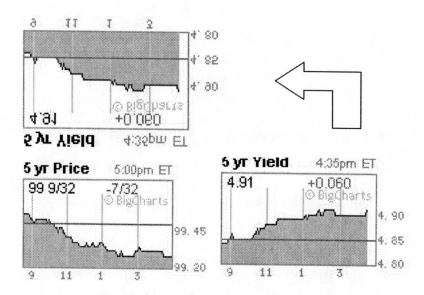

Gas prices and other inflationary catalysts have always been the nemesis of mortgage rates. When bond prices go up, rates go down; when bond prices go down, rates go up.

THE FED FUNDS RATE—an easy analogy to how it works.

Imagine Ben Bernanke, the Chairman of the Federal Reserve, is riding on top of the Budweiser beer wagon pulled by eight burly Clydesdales. The Clydesdales represent the economy. The speed they pull the wagon represents inflation. And the reins that Ben is holding represent the Fed Funds rate. As the economy heats up, and prices start to increase, Ben pulls back on the reins by raising the Fed Funds rate. That slows things down a bit and keeps the wagon moving at a controlled pace. If the economy starts to lose momentum, he lets off a little resistance and lowers the rate, allowing the horses more freedom.

FOREIGN INVOLVEMENT

The trick to this pony ride is that nearly 60% of the current purchasing of bonds is by foreign investors. This is something Chairman Ben cannot control. Visualize Ben back on his wagon in the middle of a thick fog on a road that he has never been on before. He cannot see into the future, but knows his horses well, and keeps his hands firmly on the reins. He will do his best to keep the horses moving along at a comfortable and safe pace; but cannot determine the landscape ahead. If the horses start going downhill (for example, the U.S. experiences a massive hurricane devastating the shoreline of a major metropolis corresponding with the conclusion of a war overseas, which creates thousands of new jobs and high demand for labor, increasing wages and profitability over a wide range of sectors), they will naturally have less resistance and pick up speed, and Ben reacts by pulling hard on the reins, raising interest rates sharply. If they start uphill, (For example, the U.S. freely opens its doors to China and prices of consumer products are reduced to 33 cents on the dollar, thus halting purchases of U.S. made products), he will need to let out the reins quickly to keep the horses moving or risk them coming to a dead stop.

LOCKING IN YOUR MORTGAGE

Locking in the rate on your mortgage is an essential step in the process. Because rates move up and down on a daily basis, the timing of your lock is very important. Just like a stock broker buying a stock, once you lock in the rate, the price has been set. If rates get better (a stock price fell after you bought), you cannot cancel your old lock and take the new one. And just like if rates got worse (the stock price went up after you bought), you "profit" from your timing and have a mortgage rate that is better than the current market.

PRICING LOCKS: 15, 30, 60 DAYS

Keep in mind when you are quoted your rates that they are always based on the price of a lock for a specific time frame. The standard and customary rate quote is based on a 30 day lock. Compare your rate lock to renting a storage facility. You are quoted a price based on the first month free. If you need to rent it for longer than one month (lock for greater than 30 days), you will need to pay for the additional time in blocks of 15 or 30-days. You have the opportunity to pay a fee and receive the same price as a 30-day lock, or you can take a slightly higher rate for the 60-day lock. In a later chapter you will learn which is most cost-effective, paying for a lower rate or paying nothing for a higher rate. If you only need a lock for a few days, you will receive lower rates because you only need to pay for the storage facility for the time frame you used it, which is less than one month.

**J.P Morgan, when asked what the
stock market will do, replied,
"It will fluctuate."**

TRACKING BONDS TO DETERMINE RATES

A common retort mortgage professionals have to the question, "Where are rates going?" is that "If I had that crystal ball I would be sitting on a beach somewhere! Ha Ha Ha!"

Your lender should be a little savvier.

There are several methods available to track mortgage-backed securities that help you predict which direction the price of bonds will go.

The two most prominent mortgage market analysts are Barry Habib and Sue Woodard (www.mortgagemarket-guide.com). They do a great job of analyzing market data and offering their predictions providing a technical perspective in the form of the actual bond charts updated every two minutes using "Japanese candlesticks" for you to decipher on your own, which we will cover in the next chapter. As you now understand from our gas card example from earlier, when bond prices go up, rates go down, and when bond prices go down, rates go up.

Technical analysis employs charts depicting price charts of a bond or stock as it is traded on the open market, and daily and weekly trading volumes. Pure technicians do not involve themselves with the business, competitive dynamics, valuation, growth rates, etc. Technicians use chart patterns to forecast future price movements. This book is not intended to be a lesson in Japanese candlestick patterns or technical analysis, there are numerous methods of candlestick charting, most of which are covered in "Japanese Candlestick Charting Techniques," (Steve Nison; New York Institute of Finance, New York, 1991). The basics are covered in the following graphic.

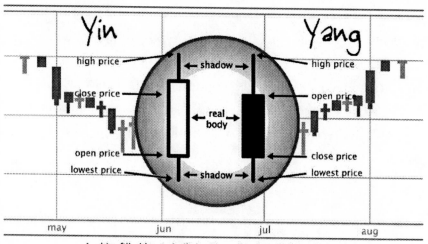

A white filled bar is bullish. The price closed above the open.
A dark filled bar is bearish. The price closed below the open.

THE BATTLE OF THE BONDS

On a daily basis, a battle takes place in the bond trading pits and the scoreboard is posted on the wall for the whole world to see in the form of a Japanese Candlestick chart (<u>www.mortgagemarketguide.com</u>). It is the traditional turf war between the bulls and the bears, both fighting to the death to gain ground. The bulls (YIN) proudly don their green as a symbol of nature, growth, harmony, freshness, fertility, and money. The bulls fight from the south, always striving to gain ground upward on the chart to increase prices and profitability. As they fight to raise prices, mortgage rates fall.

Their foe (YANG) carries red, the color of fire and blood; it is associated with energy, war, danger, strength, and power. The bears own the north and fight to lower prices and reduce profits.

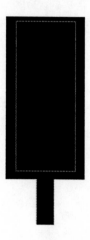

Each day the battle ensues with the creation of a new bar whose owner is yet to be determined. If green, the bulls win today's battle. If red, another day has fallen to the bears. The chart behind the current battle shows only the history of the battles previously fought indicating the current trend direction, and who currently has the current momentum of the war.

Is it the bulls driving the fighting north?

Or the bears pushing the fighting south?

Across the chart lay the trenches formed by the moving averages that serve as levels of support underneath the fighting or resistance above.

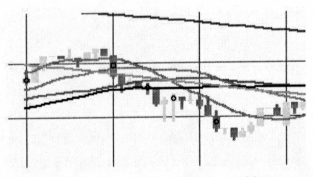

These trenches can stop the gains from either opponent. and can potentially turn the tide of the war. A great movie clip of the battle in action can be found at the intro of www.mydenverlender.com.

Of course, "the battle" tells us a lot, but it is not the answer alone. The fundamental aspects also play a big part.

"Knowledge is power."

Sir Francis Bacon (1561–1626)

FUNDAMENTAL INFORMATION

To understand the difference between pure fundamental analysis a' la **Warren Buffett** and its day-trading cousin, technical analysis, think of the market as an open-air bazaar with bonds as items for sale. A technical analyst would wade into the shopping frenzy with eyes seeking the crowd. He would ignore the goods for sale altogether.

When the trader notices a group gathering in front of the booth peddling, cookware, he'd scramble over to buy as much inventory as possible, betting that the ensuing demand would push prices higher. The trader doesn't even care what a cast iron skillet is as long as some "greater fool" at the back of the line is willing to buy it for more than the trader paid.

The fundamentalist, on the other hand, takes a more sedate approach. The fundamentalist's eyes would be solely on the products before him. He would dismiss the other shoppers as an emotional herd of fools who couldn't tell a good deal if one slapped them in the face. Once the crowd dissipated from the cookware booth, he might casually wander over to examine the merchandise.

First, the fundamentalist might try to assess the value of the metal contained in a particular skillet if melted down and sold as scrap in order to establish a base price for the object. In the bond market the value of a bond depends on the size of its coupon payments, the length of time remaining until the bond matures, and the current level of interest rates.

Next, the fundamentalist would probably take a close look at the quality of the workmanship to see if it's going to hold up over time or crack on its first use, just like a bond analyst checks a bond rating, or specification of a bond issuer's probability of defaulting based on an analysis of the issuer's financial condition and profit potential. Bond ratings start at AAA (denoting the highest investment quality) and usually end at D (meaning payment is in default). Most mortgage-backed securities are issued by Federal National Mortgage Association (Fannie Mae), the Federal Home Loan Mortgage Corporation (Freddie Mac), U.S. government-sponsored enterprises, or a small percentage issued by the Government National Mortgage Association (Ginnie Mae), a U.S. government agency, backed by the full faith and credit of the U.S. government, which guarantees that investors receive timely payments. Fannie Mae and Freddie Mac also provide certain guarantees and, while not backed by the full faith and credit of the U.S. government, have special authority to borrow from the U.S. Treasury. Some private institutions, such as brokerage firms, banks, and homebuilders, also secure mortgages, known as "private-label" mortgage securities.

Finally, the fundamentalist would combine all of the data on the asset to come up with an "intrinsic value," or a value contained in the object itself independent of the market price. Enter the economic indicators. If the market price were below the intrinsic value, meaning that there was information present to believe that the bond price was going to rise, such as poor employment data resulting in less money in the marketplace and a less profitable economy, the fundamentalist would buy it. If the market price were above the intrinsic value, as in the case when the Chairman of the Federal Reserve states they are concerned that inflation is a threat to the economy, which will reduce the vale of a bond portfolio, the fundamentalist would either sell the skillet he already owned or wait for a better deal.

The fundamentalist understands that a market investor has only two avenues in which to invest: stocks or bonds. Depending on the data that is received, the money will be invested accordingly. If indications look like the economy is clipping along, stocks are a better investment. In general stocks expose you to greater risk, but they also reap greater reward. If the economy appears strong, the risk is reduced and the greater reward still remains and the dollars go there. However, if the economy stumbles, the bonds with their low risk become more appealing, and the dollars go there.

Fundamental analysis is a lot more work, but therein lays its appeal. Crowd psychology (often considered herd mentality, because people tend to run wildly in one direction together like a spooked herd of cattle) can be a powerful yet fickle force in the markets. As a technician, you've got to stay constantly alert or risk getting trampled when the herd reverses direction, as it often does. The fundamentalist keeps a wary eye on the horizon in an effort to anticipate what will spook the herd next, and which way it will run.

For a complete list of all of the economic indicators and definitions contact a mortgage professional that subscribes to Mortgage Market Guide.

"If history repeats itself, and the unexpected always happens, how incapable must Man be of learning from experience?"

George Bernard Shaw (1856–1950)

Prologue to: A HISTORY LESSON IN MORTGAGE RATES

(I have had the good fortune to work closely with Jim McMahan, one of the mortgage industry's leading authorities on mortgage consulting over the past 20 years. This next chapter is an expansion of my research based on Jim's creation, a 200 year chart of U.S. Government Securities. The following is just a glimpse of the economic data to be found on Jim's website, *www.certifiedscripts.com*. Based on the data he has collected and interpreted, Jim has become the foremost authority on adjustable rate mortgages in the country.)

A HISTORY LESSON IN MORTGAGE RATES

The visual and timeline on the following page starts when the original GW was in office—George Washington! **Some points of interest when looking at this include:**

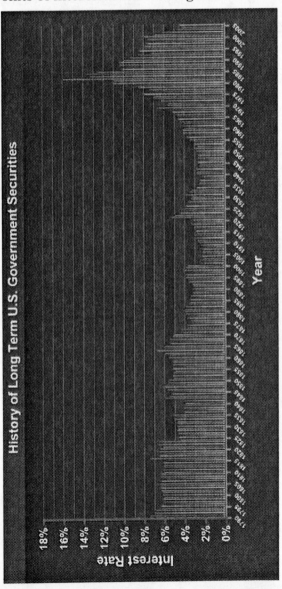

- 1945: Korea divided into US and Soviet occupation zones along 38th parallel

- 1947: President Truman's National Security Act creates US Department of Defense; **the Cold war began**

- 1950s: the United States began to send troops to Vietnam, and continued through the following 25-year period

- 1950: North Korean People's Army invades South Korea; Korean War begins

- 1953: Cease fire signed, Korean War ends

- 1956: Stalin's death; Nikita Khrushchev took over

- 1959: Fidel Castro, a Marxist, took control of Cuba.

- 1961: The Bay of Pigs Invasion

- 1962: Cuban missile crisis in October

- 1968: Soviet-led invasion of Czechoslovakia

- (1964–1982): the long rule of Leonid Brezhnev is now referred to in Russia as the "period of stagnation."

- 1972: Watergate

- October 6, 1973: the Jewish holy day of Yom Kippur, Egyptian forces attacked Israel from across the Suez Canal, while at the same time Syrian troops were flooding the Golan Heights in a surprise offensive. After early losses, Israeli counterattacks quickly pushed into Syrian territory in the north, as troops outflanked the Egyptian army in the south. Israel, **with help from the U.S.**, succeeded in reversing the Arab gains and a cease-fire was concluded in November. But on October 17, OPEC struck back against the West by imposing an oil embargo on the U.S., while increasing prices by 70% to America's Western European allies. Overnight, the price of a barrel of oil to these nations rose from $3 to $5.11. (In January 1974, they raised it further to $11.65.) The U.S. and the Netherlands, in particular, were singled out for their support of Israel in the war. When OPEC announced the sharp price rise, the shock waves were immediate. Industrial democracies, accustomed to uninterrupted sources of cheap, imported oil, were suddenly at the mercy of a modern Arab nationalism, standing up to American oil companies that had once held their countries in a vise grip. Many of these "new" Arabs were Harvard educated and familiar with the ways of the West, and to many Americans it was impossible to understand how their standard of living was now being held hostage to obscure border clashes in strange parts of the world. The embargo in the U.S. came at a time when 85% of American workers drove to their places of employment each day. Suddenly, President Nixon had to set the nation on a course of voluntary rationing. He called upon homeowners to turn down their thermostats and for companies to trim work hours. Gas stations were asked to hold their sales to a max of ten gallons per customer.

• 1973: In the month of November, Nixon proposed an extension of Daylight Savings Time and a total ban on the sale of gasoline on Sunday's. (Both were later approved by Congress.) But the biggest legislative initiative was the approval by Congress on November 13 of a Trans-Alaskan oil pipeline, designed to supply 2,000,000 barrels of oil a day. (This was completed in 1977.) A severe recession hit much of the Western world, including the U.S., and as gasoline lines snaked their way around city blocks and tempers flared (the price at the pump had risen from 30 cents a gallon to about $1.20 at the height of the crisis), conspiracy theories abounded. The rumor with the widest circulation had the whole crisis as being contrived by the major oil importers who were supposedly secretly raking in the profits. New York Harbor was really full of tankers loaded with oil, in no hurry to dock, according to the Oliver Stone/Michael Moore types. How did Wall Street respond? Well, as you might imagine shares in oil stocks performed well as profits soared, but the rest of the market swooned 15% between October 17th, 1973 and the end of November as rates continued to rocket. (The Dow Jones fell from 962 to 822.) This ended up being the middle of the great bear market that would see the Dow go from its January 11th, 1973 high of 1051 to 577 by December sixth, 1974, a whopping 45% decline over nearly two years as **mortgage rates hit 8% for the first time in American history. (You are reading correctly— 8%!)**

• 1974: Nixon resigns

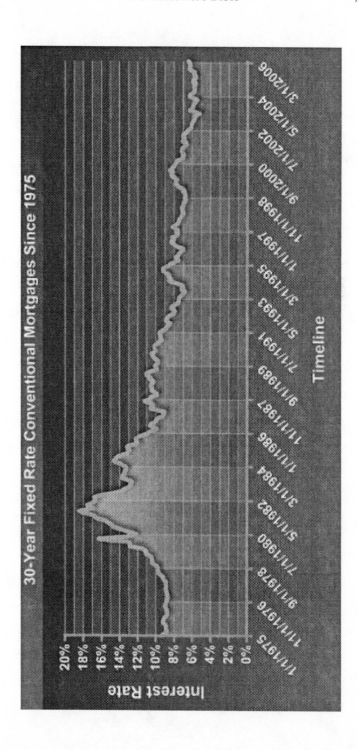

- 1977: Trans-Alaskan Oil Pipeline was completed

- 1979: the Soviet invasion of Afghanistan led to a renewal of Cold War hostility.

- 1980: Reagan elected President and the "stagflation" and "malaise" that plagued the U.S. economy from 1973 through 1980 was transformed by the Reagan economic program into a sustained period of higher growth and lower inflation.

- 1980: unemployment rate 7.0%

- 1980: The inflation rate was 10.4%

- **1980: Mortgage Rates break above 10%**

- 1981: Reagan's Program for Economic Recovery had four major policy objectives:

    (1) reduce the growth of government spending,

    (2) reduce the marginal tax rates on income from both labor and capital,

    (3) reduce regulation, and

    (4) reduce inflation by controlling the growth of the money supply.

- **1982: Mortgage rates top out above 16%**

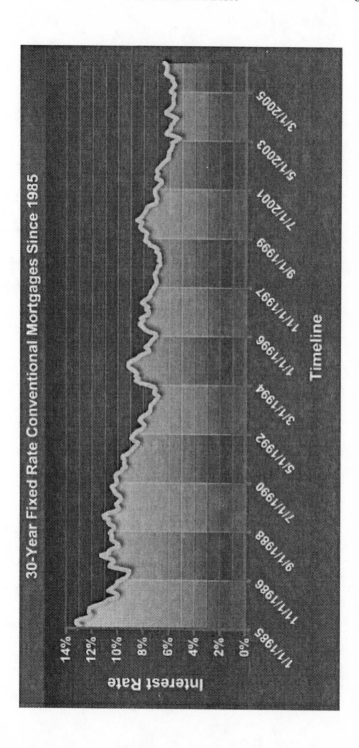

30-Year Fixed Rate Conventional Mortgages Since 1985

- 1985: Mikhail Gorbachev came to power

- **1985: Mortgage rates drop back to 10%**

- 1986: United States economy began shifting from a rapidly growing recovery to a slower growing expansion, which resulted in a "soft landing" as the economy slowed and inflation dropped. As 1987 wore on, it seemed that recessionary fears were not warranted and that boom times would continue. The stock market advanced significantly, peaking in August 1987. There were a series of volatile days that caused widespread nervousness.

- 1987: Black Monday, October 19, and October 20—The Dow suffers the biggest percentage loss in recorded stock market history on October 19 and initially continues its plunge on the 20th.

- 1988: The unemployment rate declined to 5.4%.

- 1988: The inflation rate was 4.2%.

- 1989: when the Berlin Wall came down symbolizing the end of the Cold War

- **1990: Mortgage rates reduce into single digits**

- 1991: Gulf War

- 1993: George H. W. Bush and Boris Yeltsin sign the second Strategic Arms Reduction Treaty (START).

- **1993: Mortgage Rates hit 7%**

- 1993: Bill Clinton inaugurated as President of the United States.

- **1994: Mortgage Rates exceed 8%**

- 1997: The October 27, mini-crash: the global stock market crash that was caused by an economic crisis scare in Asia. The point loss that the Dow Jones Industrial Average suffered on this day still ranks as the third biggest points loss in its 101-year existence. The crash halted trading of stocks on the New York Stock Exchange for the first time ever.

- **1998: Mortgage rates drop into the 6% range, first time since 1973.**

- 2002: Iraq's disarmament reached a crisis

- 2003: In March a coalition of primarily US and British forces invaded Iraq

- **2003: Mortgage rates drop to 5%, first time since 1967**

Notice the average interest rate prior to 1980 in the 4% range!

WHERE ARE RATES GOING?

Based on the previous chapter there is good reason to believe that the general direction of long term rates will continue to go down or remain within a range. In a speech to the Credit Union National Association in Washington during his tenure, Federal Reserve Chairman Alan Greenspan questioned whether American homeowners are well-served by popular fixed-rate long-term mortgages based on the downtrend he witnessed personally. The simple explanation of long term rates movement can be compared to a ping-pong ball bouncing down stairs. Each point of contact with the steps themselves sets a new low, then rates bounce up, but eventually fall back down and hit another, lower step. Based on the pervious chart, the most recent bounces were 1993, 1998, and 2003. Interestingly enough, they were each five years apart. If the trend continues, we could see 30-year fixed rate mortgages once again reach the 4% range sometime between 2008 and 2010.

"The only constant in the world is Change"

Ancient Greek Proverb

HOW LONG SHOULD I PLAN ON MY MORTGAGE?

Everyone's needs and lifestyles are unique, so this is the perfect question to ask your mortgage professional. The general statistics are quite compelling, however. The 2005 National Association of Realtors® Profile of Home Buyers and Sellers state that the average American sells and buys a new home once every six years, and refinances once within that time frame. That means, even if your address does not change, the way your house is financed will. For more information regarding this topic seek out a mortgage professional that subscribes to Jim McMahan's website, www.certifiedscripts.com.

HOW MUCH SHOULD I PAY FOR MY MORTGAGE?

What's the "POINT"?

This section will not overview a Good Faith Estimate and define all of the fees associated with a loan and what a customary processing fee is. That is redundant. The concept here is simple; a lender will charge you a lump sum of money up front to secure an interest rate. The more they charge up front, the lower the rate; the less they charge, the higher the rate. Period. The question you have to answer is, should I pay anything up front or not? Now it is a matter of break-even. Here is the simple equation. Let's assume that you are interested in securing an interest-only mortgage for $200,000 and the fees associated with that mortgage are $1900 for the appraisal, credit report, title work, underwriting, etc. The rate you were quoted was 6.5%, making your payment $1083 per month if you bring in $1900. You were also quoted 6.75% with a payment of $1125, and you would have the opportunity to bring in $0. A difference of $41 per month. Now the question becomes where is the break-even point? If you took the $1900 and put it in a pile, and each month you took $41 from the pile, how long would the pile last? $1900 divided by $41 equals 46.34 months. 46.34 months divided by 12 equals 3.86 years, or three years, ten months and ten days before your pile runs out.

Here is the "bet" you are about to make. You are betting the bank that you will not sell your house or change the way this loan is financed before three years and ten months. You are so sure that you are willing to "lose" $1900 today, and for the next 3.86 years, so you can begin to "win" $41 per month 3.86 years from now, at the future value of the dollar then.

Seem silly? It gets worse. The $1900 you are paying now is NOT a deductible item on your taxes (origination fees and discount points can be deducted, appraisal, credit report, etc. cannot), the $41 per month is. If you are in the 25% tax bracket, that $41 is more like $30.75 ($41–25%), making the break-even 61.78 months, or five years, one month and twenty days—even worse.

Prologue to: JUMBO LOANS VS. CONFORMING LOANS

(In 2005 I attended a seminar featuring Barry Habib and the Mortgage Market Guide, while there Barry presented the following concept to the group of 2,500 mortgage professionals and received a standing ovation. I found it so intriguing and informative that I converted it to print to share with you with Barry's permission.)

JUMBO LOANS VS. CONFORMING LOANS

Have you ever wondered why you pay more for a jumbo loan than a conforming loan amount? Why is that? If you go to Sam's Club to buy your cereal you get a deal because you are buying a bigger box. A 12-pack of Coke will cost less than 12 individual cans from the vending machine—isn't that the general rule? The more you buy the less the per unit cost right? Then WHY, when you buy a house, do you pay more for a mortgage of $500,000 than one for $250,000?!?

Here is the full circle. You walk into your lender's office to secure financing on your new home, the loan officer prepares the file for approval from the underwriter, who essentially compares your profile to secondary market guidelines to make sure the secondary market will buy your loan from them. The secondary market bundles the loans into 3, 5, 10 million dollar bundles and sells them to a variety of servicers. The servicers, who make their money off doing just that, servicing your mortgage by sending you bills, tax summaries, paying escrows, etc., doesn't hold the mortgage, they sell it to Fannie Mae or Freddie Mac, who sell it to Wall Street to be broken down into mortgage-backed securities for a fee. That fee is spread over the massive dollar amounts and passed back through the chain all the way to you as the borrower. That process takes between 30–60 days (which by no coincidence, is the same time frame your loan would traditionally be locked for prior to close). Once your loan is on the market as a mortgage-backed security who buys it? Check your 401K; if you own bonds, you own a piece of your own mortgage.

Now, on a Non-conforming loan amount, one greater than $417,000 when this was written, Fannie Mae or Freddie Mac won't touch it, so it is sold to a smaller group of investors. They follow the same circle, but when they get to the division of these quantities into mortgage-backed securities they pay the same incremental fees as Fannie Mae or Freddie Mac, but now spread over a much smaller pile of money (comparatively). Those fees are passed up the ladder through all parties and incurred in your mortgage—at a higher rate. **That** is the reason you will pay more for a larger (jumbo) loan amount than you will a smaller (conforming) loan amount.

Now for all of you type "A" analytical numbers people (All others are free to skip ahead)…Have you ever thought of the rate of return on a mortgage for an investor?   Let's keep the numbers simple and use an example of $100,000. You borrow $100,000 and secure a 5% rate on a 30-year fixed mortgage. The investor has a $5,000 rate of return on their money ($100,000 * 5% = $5,000) Then rates move to 7%.

How much money would the investor need to invest to get a $5,000 annual return now? The answer—$71,428.57. ($5,000 divided by 7%) What that means is the value of the investor's portfolio just DROPPED over 28%! If the investor wanted to earn the same $5000 with a rate of 7%, they would not need $100,000, they would only need $71,428.57. If they didn't have that money tied up with the 5% rate loan they could gain $7,000 with that same amount of money today. That's a loss of a potential 140% return. ($7,000 divided by $5,000) That's a big risk! So how do they decide where to cap their risk? The two largest investors of mortgages are Fannie Mae and Freddie Mac, whom we are all somewhat familiar with. Based on their assessment of the market, they determine their risk tolerance, currently $417,000. Anything above that loan amount falls to the smaller pool of investors.

AFTERWORD...

Thank you for reading this book. This has taken a commitment of your time and money. In return, I hope that you have gained insight on how to take control of your mortgage and make better decisions when structuring your financing.

I also hope we have an opportunity to meet someday. There is nothing more rewarding than helping contribute to another's financial freedom. Please contact me at www.baloaney.com with any questions or feedback. I am excited to receive your contact.

Keep Livin' the Dream!

ABOUT TODD...

Todd was a former high school teacher in the late 90s before he joined the mortgage profession. He has a passion to help others grow and a gift for simplifying complex topics. He has been the recipient of several awards in the mortgage industry and is invited to speak at national industry events. For more information on Todd's mortgage business, visit his mortgage website at www.mydenverlender.com.

Todd gives seminars, runs sales meetings, and conducts training programs for real estate, mortgage, and sales professionals. His passion and enthusiasm for the sales profession are contagious.

If you are interested in contacting Todd to speak to your group please contact him at www.baloaney.com.

Todd currently resides in a suburb of Denver, Colorado, with his wife and two daughters.

Printed in the United States
61407LVS00001B/289-498